Children of the World

For their help in the preparation of *Children of the World: Greece,* the editors gratefully thank Employment and Immigration Canada, Ottawa, Ont.; the US Immigration and Naturalization Service, Washington, DC; the Embassy of Greece (US), Washington, DC; the International Institute of Wisconsin, Milwaukee; the United States Department of State, Bureau of Public Affairs, Office of Public Communication, Washington, DC, for unencumbered use of material in the public domain; and Amalia Christine Panos, Milwaukee,

Library of Congress Cataloging-in-Publication Data

Hirokawa, Ryuichi, 1943-
  Greece.

  (Children of the World)
  Bibliography: p.
  Includes index.
  Summary: Presents the life of a young girl on the island of Mykonos describing her family, home, school, and amusements and some of the traditions and celebrations of her country.
  1. Greece — Social life and customs — Juvenile literature. 2. Children — Greece — Juvenile literature. [1. Greece — Social life and customs. 2. Family life — Greece. I. Sherwood, Rhoda. II. Title. III. Series: Children of the world (Milwaukee, Wis.)
DF741.H54   1988   949.5'076   87-42581
ISBN   1-55532-294-8
ISBN   1-55532-269-7 (lib. bdg.)

North American edition first published in 1988 by

Gareth Stevens, Inc.
7317 West Green Tree Road   Milwaukee, Wisconsin 53223, USA

This work was originally published in shortened form consisting of section I only.
Photographs and original text copyright © 1987 by Ryuichi Hirokawa.
First and originally published by Kaisei-sha Publishing Co., Ltd., Tokyo. World English rights arranged with Kaisei-sha Publishing Co., Ltd. through Japan Foreign-Rights Centre.

Typeset by Ries Graphics ltd., Milwaukee.
Design: Laurie Bishop and Laurie Shock.
Map design: Gary Moseley.

1   2   3   4   5   6   7   8   9   92   91   90   89   88

Children of the World

Greece

Photography by
Ryuichi Hirokawa

Edited
by
Rhoda Sherwood

Gareth Stevens Publishing
Milwaukee

. . . a note about *Children of the World*:

The children of the world live in fishing towns, Arctic regions, and urban centers, on islands and in mountain valleys, on sheep ranches and fruit farms. This series follows one child in each country through the pattern of his or her life. Candid photographs show the children with their families, at school, at play, and in their communities. The text describes the dreams of the children and, often through their own words, tells how they see themselves and their lives.

Each book also explores events that are unique to the country in which the child lives, including festivals, religious ceremonies, and national holidays. The *Children of the World* series does more than tell about foreign countries. It introduces the children of each country and shows readers what it is like to be a child in that country.

. . . and about *Greece*:

Katerina lives on beautiful Mykonos, a world-famous vacation spot. Her parents own a toy shop, where Katerina helps out after school. Mykonos, a windy island in the Aegean Sea, is a story unto itself. Here, the practice of painting all the buildings white twice a year has led to the island's nickname of "White Village."

To enhance this book's value in libraries and classrooms, comprehensive reference sections include up-to-date data about Greece's geography, demographics, language, currency, education, culture, industry, and natural resources. *Greece* also features a bibliography, research topics, activity projects, and discussions of such subjects as Athens, the country's history, political system, ethnic and religious composition, and language.

The living conditions and experiences of children in Greece vary tremendously according to economic, environmental, and ethnic circumstances. The reference sections help bring to life for young readers the diversity and richness of the culture and heritage of Greece. Of particular interest are discussions of the vast historical background of Greece and of the tremendous role Greece has played in the development of Western culture.

CONTENTS

A blue sky, a church steeple, and white houses — these are the heart of Mykonos.

LIVING IN GREECE:
Katerina, from Mykonos in the Aegean

Ten-year-old Katerina Xidakis lives on the Greek island of Mykonos, in the Aegean Sea. This famous island is called the "jewelry box" by some. It has sparkling white buildings surrounded by a deep blue sea and cloudless sky. Like many Greek children, Katerina got her name from a grandparent. Her grandmother was also called Katerina, which means "a small vinegar brewer." It is an old name on Mykonos, so Katerina's parents believe their ancestors may have been there during the Greek fight for independence in 1821.

6

"Yiasas. Ti kanete. Ime i Katerina." (Hello. How are you? I am Katerina.) Katerina with her brother, Yiorgos (YEE-or-gos); her father, Yiannis (YEE-ahn-iss); and her mother, Popi, which is a nickname for Kaliopi (Kah-lee-O-pee).

Mykonos: The White Village

The island of Mykonos has two villages, Mykonos and Ano-Mera. The port area of Mykonos, Katerina's village, is called Hora. Tourists love Mykonos. The tourist season is from April until October. In November, strong northerly winds drive the tourists away, and the 3800 residents of the island settle in for the winter.

In ancient times, a temple stood at the top of this hill.

Hora, the port, at dusk.

"ow do these buildings get so grimy?"

Manto Mavrogenous: a heroine of Mykonos who led a battle against the Turks.

What will it be — donkey or tricycle?

Tourists wander through the narrow passageways of Mykonos, riding on donkeys or motorized tricycles. Some sightsee or fish from the boats in the port. Many marvel at the sight of all the clean white buildings.

The villagers are proud of these buildings. Long ago, a king ordered that they be kept perfectly white on the outside. Now it is the village custom to whitewash them with lime twice a year. Children paint the steps and streets. Although doors and window frames may be any color, blue is quite common. Boats can also be painted any color, but roofs of churches must be red or blue.

9

Sunlight reflects off the white buildings of Mykonos, ``the jewelry box.''

Katerina lives only 160 feet (49 m) from the sea. Her house is to the left of the hill with the windmills.

Visiting Katerina's Home

Although tourists often get lost in the village passageways, Katerina knows them so well she could find her way blindfolded. In the summer, she guides tourists through the streets. Today she rushes home because the family must have dinner before Yiorgos goes to his Boy Scout meeting.

In Greece, the main meal is between noon and 2:00. The evening meal is a light snack served as late as 8:00 or 9:00 p.m.

12

Yiorgos is 12 years old and is in junior high school. He is much quieter than Katerina, so when they quarrel it is often because she teases him. Katerina loves her older brother. Sometimes she wishes she had a younger brother or sister too.

Some of these passages are so narrow that it is hard for people to pass one another.

Yiorgos shows off his Boy Scout uniform.

Popi greets Katerina as she comes in the door.

Fishermen return to Mykonos from the sea and mend their nets.

Katerina and Yiorgos climb into the family boat.

Many villagers earn their living by fishing. They bring in fish, crab, and octopus. In bad weather and in the winter, they mend their nets and repair their boats.

Yiannis, Katerina's father, is not a fisherma He and her mother, Popi, own a gift store. In the summer, while Popi takes care of the store, Yiannis uses their boat to carry tourists back and forth between the shore and large ships in the Aegean.

14

Knock on the door. Someone will appear on the porch above you and then run down to let you in.

Katerina can see the Aegean Sea from the apartment.

Katerina's house is near a *taverna*, a supper club. In the tavernas, villagers eat, drink, and dance. In the yard, the owners dry octopus, a popular food in the village. Her neighborhood also has many churches. Right in front of her house is the only Roman Catholic church on the island.

"My father makes me laugh."

The Xidakis family has a small apartment. The living room and dining room are all in one. The kitchen is connected to the dining room. Yiorgos has his own room, but Katerina has her small bed in her parents' room.

Yiannis has been in the hospital. Katerina is happy that he is feeling better. He has not been able to work, so Popi has been running the store. But he should be well by summer, in time for the tourist season. The family must earn most of its money during the tourist season because during the winter there is little work on the island.

16

Popi is a good cook. One of her best dishes is *psito chirino*, roast pork. She is also good at pickling olives and brewing wine. Some days, when Katerina helps, she gathers *horta*. Horta are dandelion greens that villagers gather from the fields for salads. Katerina washes it carefully and cuts off the roots.

Carrying the psito chirino from the kitchen.

Greek salad of cucumbers, onions, tomatoes, green peppers, and *feta* (goat cheese) — topped with olive oil.

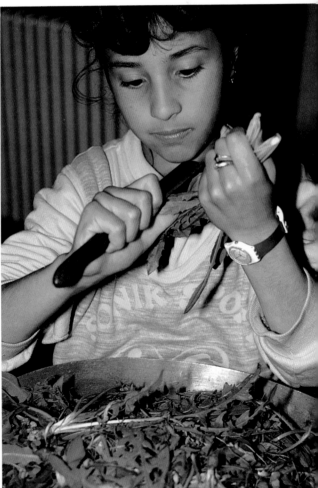

Cutting the roots of horta.

◄ Fried squid with lemon, popular on Mykonos.

17

"What a good dinner!" — Feta, rice, fresh bread, deviled eggs, peas and carrots, a Greek salad, and psito chirino.

"When we get to the shops can I buy a treat?"

Even the dogs go to market in the village!

"I want to take this home to share with Yiorgos."

Zucchini, apples, oranges, and grapefruit all look good.

A Visit to the Market

Yiannis takes Katerina to the market. In the village are tavernas, gift shops, and *cafenios*, cafes. Many of these close during the winter, but the bakery, grocery store, and fish market stay open all year so that villagers can buy what they need.

Erene (ee-REE-nee), the pelican, is a pet who has lived at the fish market for years.

Katerina loves souvlakia — roasted lamb on a skewer.

The Family Store

Near the market is the Xidakis gift shop. Katerina likes owning a store that has so many toys. She and Yiorgos save their allowances so they can buy themselves something from time to time.

On the island, workplaces are open from 8:00 to 1:30. Then everyone goes home to dinner. It is too hot to work at this time of day, so many people relax from 3:00 until 5:30, when stores reopen until 8:30.

During the summer, these hours change so that stores can be open for tourists who shop during the afternoon. In the cities, many offices are open from 8:00 until 5:00, but other urban businesses still follow the custom of closing in the afternoon.

Yiorgos asks, "Can you guess what the Greek letters mean above the door?"

Katerina visits Yiannis one evening when he reopens the store.

When Yiannis was in the hospital, Katerina helped run the shop after school. She now knows how much everything costs and how to use the cash register. Yiannis cannot work long hours, so he has time to talk with friends in the cafenio that is near the novelty shop.

Cafenios are important to Greek social life. People gather there to talk, play backgammon, and enjoy a cup of thick coffee or a glass of *ouzo*. Ouzo is a popular Greek liqueur that turns cloudy white when mixed with water. An afternoon with friends in the cafenio gives men a break from their winter work. Most days they keep busy mending nets, repairing boats, and reading.

Another social custom is the promenade, especially in small towns. In the evening, villagers walk up and down the main street, talking with friends until tavernas and cafenios close.

23

Katerina looks forward to seeing her friends at school.

She enters the courtyard of her school.

Katerina's School

At 7:30 Popi wakes Katerina for school. After washing her face and getting dressed, Katerina drinks a glass of milk and brushes her teeth. Sometimes, if she wakes up early, she studies in the morning. She leaves for school at 8:20. Since school is only a 3-minute walk away, she will be on time for her first class at 8:30.

"This is the door to my classroom."

Before classes begin, students rush to the playground so they can catch up on the news and play for a while. Katerina loves to run and dance. She also likes small children, so she is thinking about being a ballet teacher or kindergarten teacher when she grows up.

"Did anyone remember to bring a basketball?"

Before class, a student prays and everyone makes the sign of the cross.

Katerina's class poses on the playground. Katerina is fifth from the left, kneeling.

Katerina is in school from 8:30 to 12:30. She studies the Greek language, math, science, ethics, and music. But the subjects she most enjoys are drawing, crafts, and myths and legends of Greece. At midmorning, the students take a break. Katerina eats sandwiches Popi has made or buys baked goods at the school snack bar. Then she runs to the playground for a few minutes before classes begin again.

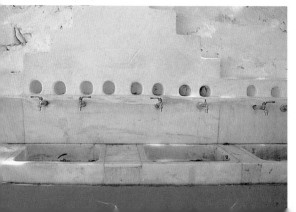

e basins in the school are made of marble taken from earby hills long ago.

"Stretch those arms or you'll never play on our Olympic basketball team."

There are three elementary schools on the island. Katerina's is the largest, with 400 students and 14 teachers. The school in Ano-Mera has 60 students, and a branch school further away has 10 students. Katerina's building has only 12 classrooms, so some students must attend school in the afternoon.

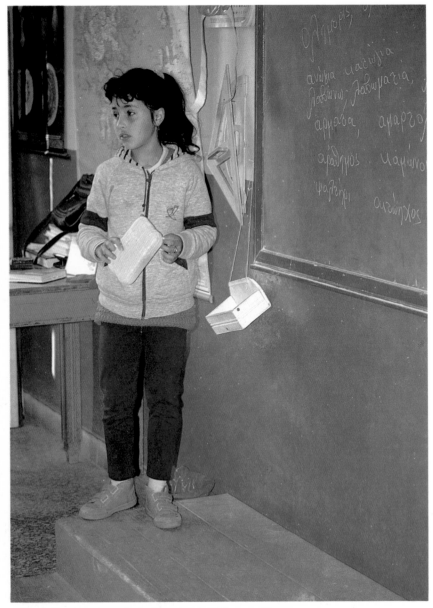

Her fellow students help Katerina with her spelling.

The Aegean Sea provides beautiful shells for the students.

Katerina's sketch of a famous church on Mykonos, the Church of Paraportiani.

s. Papanopoulos teaches all Katerina's subjects. She is good-natured — unless the students are noisy.

Having Fun After School

On most days, Katerina arrives home from school at 1:10. She puts her bookbag down, gives her parents a kiss, washes her hands, and helps her mother in the kitchen. After dinner, she helps her mother clear the dishes from the table. The adults then rest. Children would much rather go out to play. Yiorgos and Katerina have many kinds of activities that they enjoy.

Katerina walks up to the second-floor apartment. Pots of flowers line these steps in the summer.

One of Katerina's favorite activities is English class. Because the elementary school has no English language classes, Katerina studies English in the evening twice a week. Other children who also want to learn English join her in this special class.

Sometimes Katerina must study after school. She is a girl who loves to play, so she has to discipline herself to get her school work done before she runs outside to find friends and mischief. Mrs. Papanopoulos, her teacher, says that Katerina is the best at everything — except studying.

"...he English alphabet doesn't look like Greek to me."

"I use my eraser a lot when I have hard homework."

Katerina and Yiorgos have a lot of energy. They are interested in every activity children can take part in on the island. Some days they go to a shop where they can play backgammon. They want to be as skilled as the men who play at the cafenio.

"Okay, you win this one. Let's make it two out of three."

"I don't think I've had quite enough fun yet. What else is planned?"

Katerina also attends Girl Scout meetings once a week. She likes the troop leader, who is the mother of one of the girls in the group. At the meetings, Katerina learns about the history of the Girl Scouts. The girls also earn badges by doing chores and running errands for villagers. Katerina's favorite meetings are those when her leader plans a special day of fun for everyone.

Katerina's grandmother knows how to do traditional Greek weaving, so Katerina often visits her for lessons. Besides teaching her how to weave, Katerina's grandmother tells her stories about the history of Greece. Many of these stories are about unhappy days for the Greek people. For 400 years, Turkey controlled Greece. Greeks gained their independence from the Turks in 1821.

During World War II, the Germans took over Greece. When they were driven out, a Greek military government ruled the people. Under military rule, Greeks suffered because leaders took away much of their freedom and people were very, very poor. Katerina and her grandmother are both happy that those days are gone. Today Greece has a government elected by the people.

Katerina practices on her grandmother's loom.

Like children all over the world, Katerina has special toys.

A Greek Orthodox priest rings the bells of his church.

Greek Traditions

Religion is very important to the Greek people. In Katerina's small village, there are 365 churches — one for every 10 residents.

The most famous of these is Paraportiani. It is large and white on the outside. It is filled with detailed painting, sparkling lights, and gold decoration. While it is an impressive church, Katerina likes the smaller churches scattered throughout the island.

raportiani Church glitters with gold paint and fine paintings of religious figures.

Yiannis and Popi light a candle in the family chapel.

On the first floor of the Xidakis house is the family chapel. On special religious days, the family lights a candle here. The names of ancestors are written on the walls, and their bones are kept here.

About 98% of the Greek people belong to the Eastern Orthodox Church, also called the Greek Church. The Eastern Orthodox faith is the official religion of Greece. Students learn the beliefs of this faith in school, and the government supports its priests. Priests may marry in the Greek Church, but they will not be able to get high offices if they do.

Beginning in 1054, Christianity had two branches. The eastern had its head in Constantinople, now Istanbul, Turkey. The western had its head in Rome. The two branches split because they disagreed about some beliefs. Katerina's church has been called the Eastern Orthodox Church since that time, and the western branch is now the Roman Catholic Church.

Myths about their past are also important to Greeks. One myth says that Mykonos is the island where Hercules killed and buried a giant. Near Mykonos is the island of Delos. Greek legend says that the sun god Apollo and the moon goddess Artemis were born on Delos. At one time slave traders used it as a market. Now much of the island is full of ruins.

For decades, archeologists have been digging all over Greece, looking for signs of the earlier peoples who lived in this ancient country.

At the end of the harbor is a museum filled with pieces found from earlier civilizations.

ancient Greece, an artist painted enes about daily life and important tles on vases, bowls, and plates.

Remains of ancient statues found on Mykonos and Delos.

"Come on, let's do the sirtaki."

Like other Greek children, Katerina is learning the folk dances. Often, she and her friends practice these dances before school. Katerina likes ballet, but she enjoys these traditional dances too.

Katerina and her best friend, Sophia, practice a difficult step

One popular folk dance is the *sirtaki*. Katerina once won a medal in a contest. Musicians play the *bouzouki* while dancers go through the steps. The bouzouki is a stringed instrument that resembles a mandolin. It was originally brought to Greece many years before by Turkish invaders.

On March 25th, Greece celebrates independence from Turkey. After a parade in Mykonos, Katerina and some friends will perform a Greek folk dance. She is looking forward to dancing for her friends and family.

Greeks are pleased when visitors to their country want to try native folk dances with them. It is a sign of friendship and of interest in the Greek people.

Katerina dresses up like a Greek princess.

"I wonder if Sophia is ready for school yet."

Katerina's Special Pleasures

Many mornings, on her way to school, Katerina stops to pick up her friend Sophia. Sophia is the tallest girl in class, and Katerina is the shortest. Sometimes the two laugh about the differences in their size.

They have been classmates and best friends since first grade. They are in the same Girl Scout troop, and they like to wander through the narrow streets of the village, chattering with one another about school and friends. They quarrel, as all friends do, but one of them always makes up. They hope to go to college together someday.

Before Lent, Katerina and Yiorgos take part in a parade.

Katerina loves Easter season. Greeks devote more time to Lent and Easter than they do to Christmas. For three weeks before Lent, they celebrate with a carnival period of eating, drinking, and dancing. People dress up in costumes and have parties and parades. On the final night of celebrating, the last food they eat is eggs.

Some people are not as interested in costumes as Katerina

The next day, the first day of Lent, is Holy Monday, also called "Clean Monday." It is a day of rest after celebration. The tradition is to go on picnics and to fly kites. On this day, Greeks eat no meat. Instead, they eat vegetables and any seafood other than fish. They also eat an unleavened bread called *lagana*. For the next seven weeks, they fast. Then the first food eaten on Easter is eggs they have dyed red.

Priests and villagers parade through the streets.

On Clean Monday, the people of Ano-Mera carry a picture called an ikon down the hill to Mykonos village. It will stay there until Easter. Ikons, which are important in many religions, are special pictures or carvings of Jesus, the Virgin Mary, or a saint.

The ikon stays in the church until Easter.

43

On Clean Monday, the Xidakis family visits their new home in Ano-Mera.

annis was born in and grew up in this house.

"I wonder if this well still has clean, fresh water."

ople once spread grain on the ground here and husked by stepping on it.

If you take a winding slope away from the harbor and drive by car for 20 minutes in the direction of the Mykonos airport, you will reach the house where Yiannis was born. After Yiannis's father died, his mother moved to the village, so no one has lived in the house for years. It is being fixed up so that Katerina's family can move in.

Yiannis is happy to be moving back to his family home. He prefers the wide-open village to the crowded harbor. Katerina also loves the open fields. Here, the family can raise chickens, sheep, and donkeys. When her grandfather was alive, the fields were sown with wheat. Katerina hopes that once the family moves here, she will work the land with her parents and brother. She wants her grandmother to visit often.

On Clean Monday, Yiannis flies his kite at his childhood home.

45

A Special Treat — A Party at the Taverna

Katerina has more than 50 relatives on Mykonos. Some are sailors and hotel managers. Popi's older brother, Uncle Petro, owns a taverna called *Tin Thalasa,* The Sea.

On a Friday or Saturday night, the family often gathers at Uncle Petro's taverna to eat, sing, and dance. On special occasions like these, Katerina and Yiorgos are allowed to stay up late — even until 2:00 in the morning.

Katerina sits next to Uncle Petro, the owner of Tin Thalasa.

"I can hardly wait to show this one to Sophia."

Katerina dances with the grown-ups. She is learning new steps and is eager to teach them to Sophia and other girls in school. Katerina knows that she is lucky to be living on a beautiful island surrounded by a deep blue ocean. She is lucky to be moving to a farm. But especially she is lucky to have an uncle who owns a taverna where she can dance and dance and dance.

FOR YOUR INFORMATION: Greece

Official Name: Hellenic Republic
Elliniki Dimokratia (el-ee-NEE-kee dee-mah-krah-TEE-ah)

Capital: Athens

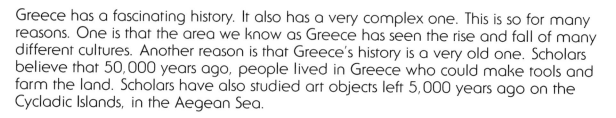

History

Greece has a fascinating history. It also has a very complex one. This is so for many reasons. One is that the area we know as Greece has seen the rise and fall of many different cultures. Another reason is that Greece's history is a very old one. Scholars believe that 50,000 years ago, people lived in Greece who could make tools and farm the land. Scholars have also studied art objects left 5,000 years ago on the Cycladic Islands, in the Aegean Sea.

The Minoans and Mycenaeans

Asiatic people who landed on Crete, just south of mainland Greece, set up the first

Athens, the capital of Greece. Mt. Lykavitos rises up in the background.

state in Europe 3,000 years ago. These were the Minoans, named after their king, Minos. A rather advanced bronze age culture, they built the palaces and temples at Knossos. You can still see the ruins of these buildings. The Minoans lasted about 1,500 years, until 1450 BC Mycenaeans, another advanced civilization, lived on mainland Greece. They were the people who fought the Trojan War described in Homer's *The Iliad* and *The Odyssey*. These poems tell how Troy, in modern Turkey, fell to the Mycenaeans around 1200 BC. From 1900 BC on, waves of tribes had been invading Greece. The Dorians were one of the later tribes. A crude, iron age civilization, they destroyed much that the Mycenaeans had created.

The Classical Period

From 750-500 BC, Greek city-states grew around the Mediterranean and Black seas. These city-states were called *polis*, from which we get our word for a city, *metropolis*. Members of a city-state shared language, values, religion, legends, sports, and governmental institutions. They competed in the Olympic games, begun about 776 BC. When a city-state became crowded, people moved to a new area but kept ties to the parent state. Dominant city-states were Athens, Sparta, and Thebes. In the 6th century, Persia, which is modern Iran, began threatening Greece. City-states united for war.

The Golden Age

From 546 to 479 BC, Greece fought Persia. Finally, Greece won and enjoyed peace from 479 to 431 BC. During these 48 years, Greece experienced a great burst of culture. Teachers, artists, and government leaders developed ideas that have directly affected Western thinking. But then Sparta and Athens began to fight about who was going to control Greece. The Golden Age was over. The Peloponnesian War (431-404 BC) between Sparta and Athens ended with Athens defeated. But all of Greece suffered because a northern Greek tribe, the Macedonians, invaded the weakened country.

The Byzantine Empire

Philip II and his son, Alexander the Great, led that tribe. The two ruled Greece from 357 to 323 BC. Philip was the first military man to use horses in battle rather than as pack animals. With Philip's murder in 336 BC, Alexander took control. For the next 13 years, he led 40,000 soldiers east into Persia and settled in Byzantium, in modern Turkey. Alexander never returned. He died in Babylon when only 33. But in his brief life, he spread Greek ideas east and south to northern Africa. Alexandria, a city in Egypt named after him, became the cultural center of the Greek world.

Invasions by Romans and Christians

For the next 123 years, native warlords controlled Greece. Then Romans invaded. They conquered Greece in 146 BC. In 324 AD, with the weakening of the Roman

Empire, the first Christian emperor, Constantine, split the empire into two parts. The eastern capital was in Byzantium. But first, Constantine named the city after himself, calling it Constantinople. The city is now named Istanbul. Constantine made Christianity the official religion and got rid of many rituals and temples used in the worship of gods and goddesses. Later rulers also banned the ancient religion.

Ottoman Domination

From 620 to the 1400s, many tribes ransacked Greece. First, it was the Goths, Vandals, Huns, and Slavs. From the 10th to 14th centuries, it was Bulgarians, Franks, and Italians. Finally, Ottoman Turks took Constantinople and ruled Greece. The Muslim Turks did not impose their faith on the Christian Greeks. During Turkish rule, Christians in Constantinople broke with the Christians in Rome. That break exists to this day. Now Greeks follow the teachings of the Eastern Orthodox Church while Western Catholics follow the beliefs of the Roman Catholic Church.

Modern Greece

From 1821 to 1829, Greece fought for independence from the Turks. Once free, they put royalty on the throne again, until 1926, when a military dictator took control. In 1941, the Germans invaded. They were driven out in 1944. But then Communists and Nationalists began fighting. Greeks tortured and killed other Greeks. About 80,000 died, and another 700,000 were chased from their homes by their countrymen. The Nationalists won, and royalty were once again in power. Until 1975, control of Greece passed back and forth between royalty and the military.

In July 1974, a crisis occurred in the nearby Republic of Cyprus, an island settled by both Greek and Turkish Cypriots. Greek officers with their Greek-Cypriot army tried to murder the president of Cyprus, Archbishop Makarios, and take over Cyprus. This angered the Turks, who invaded Cyprus a week later. Threatened by war, the Greek military backed down and resigned. The civilian cabinet that took control freed political prisoners and cooperated with Turkey over Cyprus. Greece held elections in November 1974, and one month later passed the constitution making the country a republic. In 1975, power passed to elected officials, and the current royal family, the Glyksburgs, went into exile in England.

Government

Greece is so old that it has been said Greeks have tried every form of government the world has known. In tavernas, cafes, and homes, they happily argue about politics and politicians.

Greece now is a presidential parliamentary republic. The executive branch consists of the president, prime minister, and cabinet. Parliament elects the president, who holds a five-year term and can be reelected once. Advising the president is the Council of the Republic. The president appoints the prime minister and the cabinet, but parliament must approve of these appointments. The three major parties in Greece are the Panhellenic Socialist Movement (PASOK), the New Democracy (ND), and the Communist Party (KKE-Exterior).

In 1980, Greece became a full member of the North Atlantic Treaty Organization, NATO. In 1981 it became the tenth full member of the European Economic Community, EEC. But Greece actually conducts its foreign policy with an eye to both East and West and becomes angry at anyone who interferes too much in Greek affairs. Recently, Greece has complained about US support of Turkey in the Greek-Turkish quarrel over Cyprus. For its part, the US hasn't liked Greece's friendship with the USSR or its attitude toward NATO troops and bases in Greece.

The People — Population and Ethnic Groups

Greece has suffered from poverty and military invasions since World War I. By 1950, 10% of the Greek people had starved or died in war. In 1984, Greece had a population of 9,900,000. About 94% of the people are Greek, and 4% are Turks. The remainder are Slav, Albanian, Armenian, and Bulgarian. The Greek Orthodox Church and the Greek language are important to the people because both help Greeks see themselves as a united nation.

Most Greeks live in cities along the plain of Attica, on the plains of Thrace, on the western coast of the Peloponnese, and in the Ionian Islands. Poverty has driven many people to cities such as Athens and to industrial centers in Western Europe, Canada, the US, and Australia, in search of jobs.

Men and women have different amounts of freedom in Greece. Men more often go to cafes and move freely in society. Women keep closer ties to home before they marry. If a woman's husband dies, she is expected to wear black for the rest of her life. More men than women can read and write. There are fewer men than women in Greece, so many American Greeks send money back to young women who live in Greece so that they will have a dowry that will attract a husband.

Language

Although people in many regions speak their own dialects, most Greeks speak Demotic Greek. It became the official language after 1977. The Greek alphabet has some letters that readers of English would recognize: A, E, I, K, M, N, T, Y, and Z. But other letters are not like those in English. They are π (P), Ξ (X), Δ (D), Γ (G), Λ (L), Ω (O), Σ (S), Θ (TH), Φ (PH), and Ψ (PS).

Education

Taxes fund education from grade school through college, paying for tuition as well as books. Since 1980, the government has required students to go to high school, and about 80% graduate. Elementary school lasts six years. Secondary school is divided into two parts: each lasts 3 years. Students must attend the first three years, when they receive a general education. Those who attend the second three choose a general, classical, or technical-professional education. After high school, students may attend the university for four to six years. Twice as many men as women go on for more schooling after high school.

Currency

The drachma is the basic monetary unit. It is made up of 100 lepta. Drachmas are divided into 1, 2, 5, 10, 20, and 50 units. Bills are in quantities of 50, 100, 500, 1,000, and 5,000 drachmas.

Industry

The German occupation during World War II and the civil war after 1944 wrecked the Greek economy. In 1948, it began to recover. Little land is farmed in Greece, so the economy rests primarily on shipbuilding, shipping, and tourism. Greece is famous for its international shipping industry. Its merchant navy may be the largest in the world. About 80% of the goods go to ports in the Aegean. Major exports are textiles, metal products, cement, chemicals, and pharmaceuticals.

"Invisible earnings" are another source of income for Greeks. This means that young Greek men go abroad to work and then send money home to family members. After a few years, the men return to Greece and set up tourist businesses. Tourism is the major Greek industry. Over 6 million visitors a year spend over $500 million yearly on their visits. Athens, on the mainland, is a tourist center, as are islands such as Corfu, Rhodes, Crete, and Mykonos.

Agriculture

Greece is so rocky, mountainous, or swampy that farmers can use only 30% of the land, 15,300 sq miles (39,627 sq km). This is an area the size of West Virginia and smaller than Nova Scotia. About 25% of the population works in farming. Most farms are about 25 acres (10 hectares). But since World War II, some farms have gotten larger because farmers are combining smaller farms and draining marshes. Some now use better fertilizers. In very remote areas, farm families might raise only enough food to feed themselves. The seasonal breezes, called *meltemia*, and the consistently sunny days make Greece a perfect place for vineyards. Major crops are wheat, maize, barley, grapes, lemons, olives, and, more recently, rice.

Sheep and goats appear all over Greece, grazing low on hills in winter and high in pastures in summer. Most Greek farmers still rely on donkeys for plowing and carrying goods because the hills are too rocky for tractors, although in Thrace (northern Greece) farmers substitute oxen and horses as draft animals. Farmers raise poultry, sheep, goats, and pigs. Cattle are not commonly raised.

Natural Resources

Greece is not rich in natural resources. Its people and its setting are its greatest resources. But it does have nickel, copper, iron, zinc, and coal, as well as aluminum plants and marble and limestone quarries.

Greeks have been tied to the sea because of Greece's many miles of coastline, so the seas are another resource. Fish are a staple in the Greek diet. Despite increasing pollution, the seas provide mullet, sardines, and tuna. Some Greeks work in the sponge industry.

Land

Greece dips into the Mediterannean Sea east of Italy. To the west is the Ionian Sea, and to the east is the Aegean Sea. Its total land area is 50,994 sq miles (131,944 sq km), about the size of Alabama or of Nova Scotia and New Brunswick combined. But 9,000 sq miles (23,000 sq km) of this land is in Greece's 1,400 islands. To the north of Greece are the Communist countries of Yugoslavia, Albania, and Bulgaria. To the northeast lies Greece's ancient enemy, Turkey. Just across the Mediterranean is Africa.

Seven major Greek islands lie in the Ionian Sea. Many more are in the Aegean. Because of coasts around all the islands and the mainland, the entire coastline of this small country totals over 9300 miles (15,000 km). This is the longest shoreline in Europe. Living so close to the ocean has made Greeks a seafaring people.

Many Greek islands are tips of ancient mountain ranges that shift and move because of forces inside the earth. In the Aegean Sea, Santorini and Samos still have active volcanoes. About 80% of Greece is mountainous. Once the land was more fertile than it is. But people have lived in Greece for 50,000 years, and many were not careful with the land. For centuries, farmers cleared forests and let their animals graze until the roots of plants were gone. Without roots to hold soil in place, rain washed earth down the valleys and into the seas.

Today, for the most part, the land is rocky and barren, with white limestone and red soil.

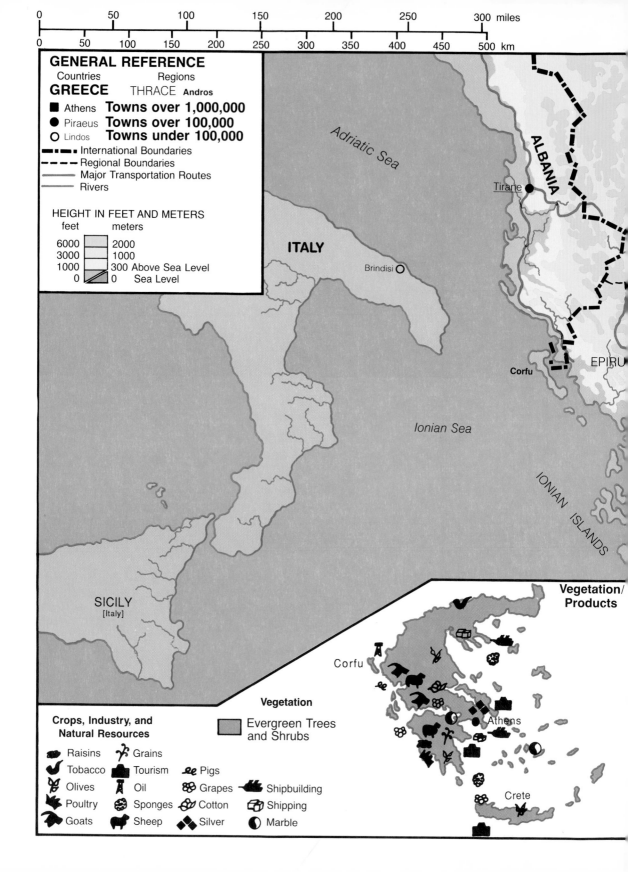

Scale bar (top):
0 — 50 — 100 — 150 — 200 — 250 — 300 miles
0 — 50 — 100 — 150 — 200 — 250 — 300 — 350 — 400 — 450 — 500 km

GENERAL REFERENCE

Countries   Regions

GREECE   THRACE   Andros

■ Athens   **Towns over 1,000,000**
● Piraeus   **Towns over 100,000**
○ Lindos   **Towns under 100,000**
▪■▪■ International Boundaries
▪ ▪ ▪ Regional Boundaries
—— Major Transportation Routes
—— Rivers

HEIGHT IN FEET AND METERS

feet	meters	
6000	2000	
3000	1000	
1000	300	Above Sea Level
0	0	Sea Level

Adriatic Sea

ALBANIA

Tirane ●

ITALY

Brindisi ○

Corfu

EPIRU

Ionian Sea

IONIAN ISLANDS

SICILY
[Italy]

**Vegetation/
Products**

Corfu

Athens

Vegetation

☐ Evergreen Trees
and Shrubs

Crete

Crops, Industry, and Natural Resources

Raisins	Grains	Pigs
Tobacco	Tourism	Grapes
Olives	Oil	Cotton
Poultry	Sponges	Silver
Goats	Sheep	

Shipbuilding	
Shipping	
Marble	

Black Sea

BULGARIA

Rhodope Mts.

OSLAVIA

Istanbul

Nestos

THRACE

Sea of Marmara

Strumon

MACEDONIA

Thessaloniki

AYION OROS

Ikmon

Mount Olympus
9568 ft / 2917 m

Mount Athos
6670 ft / 2033 m

Limnos

TURKEY

THESSALY

Aegean Sea

Lesbos

E

Sperkhios

MTS.

Mount Parnassos
8059 ft / 2467 m

EUBOEA

Khios

RAL

GREECE

Plain of
Attica

Andros

Gulf of Corinth

Piraeus

Patrai

Athens

inios

Corinth

Mykonos

PELOPONNESE

Cyclades Islands

Sparta

Milos

Rhodes

Lindos

Dodecanese Islands

Mediterranean Sea

Iraklion

CRETE

Climate

Southern Greece, the island of Crete, and the Aegean Islands have mild winters and long, dry summers. The temperatures may reach 55°F (13°C) in winter and 92°F (33°C) in July. But many summer days, it is cloudfree and over 100°F (38°C). In the summer of 1987, over 500 people, primarily the elderly, died during a prolonged heat wave. Winter and fall are rainy. Western Greece gets the most rain and, occasionally, cyclones. Northern Greece, made up of Macedonia, Thessaly, and Thrace, enjoys a moderate climate, with cool summer temperatures. Winter temperatures can drop to 48°F (9°C), and snow will appear on mountain peaks.

Religion

The Gods and Goddesses

The Ancient Greeks believed in gods and goddesses who supposedly lived on Mount Olympus. There were 12 major gods and goddesses and some lesser figures. The king of the gods was Zeus. With him on Mount Olympus were, among others, his wife, Hera; their son, Apollo; Poseidon, god of the sea; Hephaestus, god of fire; Athena, goddess of wisdom; Aphrodite, goddess of beauty and love; and Ares, god of war. These Olympian gods appear in literature, painting, and sculpture created throughout the centuries.

Christianity

About 97% of the people belong to the Greek branch of the Eastern Orthodox Church, known as the Greek Church or the Greek Orthodox Church. The remainder are Muslims, Jews, or Roman Catholic and Protestant Christians. On Athos peninsula, in Thessaly, are 20 Byzantine monasteries. The Greek government allows the monks living there to govern themselves according to religious law. Only men may live or visit there, and non-orthodox males need permission to stay overnight. Chickens and female cats are the only females allowed on monastery land.

Easter — A Major Greek Celebration

Greeks devote nearly three months to celebration of Easter. For three weeks preceding Lent, there is a carnival atmosphere. On the last Sunday before Lent, everyone visits friends. The last food they eat before Lent begins is eggs. The next day, Shrove Monday (called "Clean Monday" by Greeks), is spent picnicking and flying kites in the countryside. No one eats meat, only seafood, vegetables, and *lagana*, an unleavened bread.

For the seven weeks of Lent, no one eats animal products. Throughout the week before Easter, many women wear black, no one entertains, and churches hold services twice a day. On Good Friday, no one works or eats. Flags fly at half-mast. On Saturday night before Easter Sunday, everyone attends church and celebrates Christ's resurrection. People then return home and feasting begins. At 3:00 on the afternoon of Easter Sunday, everyone gathers in church for the "Service of Love." They hear gospel passages read in many languages to show the unity of all people. The celebration of Easter continues for three more days. In total, then, Greeks devote nearly three months to Easter activities.

Greece — the Birthplace of Western Culture

This tiny but ancient country has given us many of our ideas about art, literature, science, justice, liberty, and law. The first libraries in the West began because of people like Demetrius Phalereus, a Greek who planned the library at Alexandria for one of the Ptolemy kings of Egypt. As you go through school, you will learn about other brilliant Greeks.

For instance, lawyers learn about Solon, the Lawgiver, who lived in Greece in the 6th century BC. He set up democratic laws and freed people who had been made slaves just because they owed someone money. Playgoers will see the works of Aeschylus, Sophocles, Euripides, and Aristophanes. Even though these men wrote 2300 to 2500 years ago, their plays remain popular. Two of the earliest histories we know were written in the 5th century BC — *Peloponnesian War*, by Thucydides, and *Persian Wars*, by Herodotus (who is known as the "father of history").

The first medical school in the West may have been set up by Hippocrates. Now, as part of their medical training, doctors recite the Hippocratic Oath. Well-read stargazers will know about Meton, one of the world's first astronomers. Finally, many college students learn about the philosopher, Socrates; his student, Plato; and Aristotle, one of the first Westerners to organize learning into an orderly system. One of the young men at Aristotle's school in Athens was Alexander the Great. Some people believe that these men have influenced not only what we Westerners think about but *how* we think.

Arts

Architecture

Many people admire classical Greek architecture. They are fascinated by the ancient ruins, built in special places for spiritual reasons. On Crete are the remains of Knossos, the palace of King Minos, built in 1700 BC and destroyed in 1400 BC. Around the palace are priests' rooms, burial grounds, and homes for citizens. At Bassae, in the Peloponnese, is a temple built about 450-425 BC by Ictinus, a designer of the Parthenon. Much of this temple remains, perhaps because it is high in the mountains. In Athens, four buildings remain of the ancient Acropolis, built in

57

the 5th century BC during the Golden Age of Greece. In many churches and monasteries, visitors can see the influence of the Turks in the elaborate detail of Byzantine architecture.

Sculpture

You don't need to visit Greece to see its sculpture. This is because non-Greeks raided Greece and carried pieces back to museums in their countries. In the 1st century AD, Nero took many statues to Rome, and in the 19th century, Lord Elgin took entire carvings off the Parthenon and shipped them to the British Museum in London. In 1801, English collectors shipped a statue of the goddess Demeter to Fitzwilliam Museum in Cambridge, England. Over the centuries, many statues have been found in the sea and in the earth.

The Parthenon, in Athens.

Scholars have been carefully cleaning and repairing these pieces and then placing them in museums. Greeks are famous in the world of art for their ability to capture the beauty and power of the human form.

Paintings

Early Greek painting is seen on the vases, plates, bowls, and jars made by potters. After completing their pieces, potters painted on them scenes from war, daily life, and the lives of the gods. Many churches and monasteries show the influence of Turkish rule in the detailed paintings and mosaics on their walls, floors, and ceilings.

Handicrafts

Like their sisters in ancient times, modern Greek women weave, embroider, and knit. On the islands, the products of these domestic arts are an important part of a family's income. Peasant women in Attica embroider costumes, purses, and dresses. Women on Crete and Rhodes make laces. Arachova is known for the rugs, bedspreads, and linens made by local women. On Skyros, some pieces are displayed in museums. Handicraft works of art are so important to Greeks that women attend the "Royal Greek Handicraft Schools" in order to learn traditional and modern designs.

Music

Although Greece has an ancient culture, it does not have the history of musical accomplishment other European cultures do. This may be because Turkey controlled

Greece during the 400 years when developments in music occurred on the rest of the continent.

In classical Greece, language was so intertwined with music that the same word, *mousike*, stood for both music and poetry. Greek males learned melody, harmony, and rhythm. Before writing appeared, singers, or bards, recited the history of the people at special gatherings. They memorized stories about their people.

A Greek folk dance.

The Olympic Games — Another "First" for Greece

The Olympic Games were first held in Olympia, on the Peloponnesian peninsula, in 776 BC. By 676 BC, Greeks from areas outside Olympia came to compete. Games were held every four years, from June until September. To announce the games, men ran from village to village. For centuries, winners did not get gifts, trophies, or medals. The only reward was an olive wreath placed on the head. Sometimes statues were made of winners.

By 150 BC, Olympia had lost some of its glory. When Christianity became the official religion, statues and other stonework of the original Olympic site became part of a castle. In 393 AD, Emporer Theodosius I banned the games, and in 426 AD, his son, Theodosius II, destroyed the temples. The Goths who came later nearly finished off the buildings. And in the following centuries, the Kladeos River changed course twice, covering the land with dirt. But archeologists uncovered Olympia in 1975.

The modern Olympics began in 1896 because the Frenchman Pierre de Coubertin (1863-1937) thought the games would show people the benefits of competition that followed ancient Greek ideals. Now, Greek athletes are first in the parade held before the games begin. A runner carrying a torch leads the parade. He represents the early runner who announced the games to the Greek villagers. The flame in the torch still comes from Olympia. Runners carry it to the site of the current games. When the Olympics are held in the Western Hemisphere, this means carrying the flame by airplane. But in 1976, a satellite beamed the flame to Ottawa, and runners carried it to Montreal, the site of the games that year.

Women first competed in 1904, in archery. Then, in 1908, they competed in tennis. In 1912, the Olympic committee added swimming to the women's games, and in

1928, they added track and field games. Since then, women have competed in such sports as gymnastics, skiing, skating, volleyball, and basketball.

In ancient Greece, squabbling city-states would stop briefly so they could compete. The games became a way to encourage unity among Greeks — if only for a short period. In modern times, too, most countries send athletes, despite quarrels. But recently, governments have prevented their athletes from competing when they were angry at another country.

Athens

Athens, the capital of Greece, is densely populated, with 1,980,000 people. In the 5th century BC, Athens was a major city, but invading Goths destroyed it. During the Byzantine Empire, Christians erected some shrines, but no real building took place until after 1834, when Greece gained independence from Turkey and Athens became the capital. Now it is a modern city. Much of it was planned by German architects and finished by 1950. In the 60s and 70s, it became more industrial. People rushed there in search of jobs. New neighborhoods are not as well planned as earlier ones, and pollution has become so serious that it is eating away at the ruins of the ancient Acropolis in central Athens. Other famous ruins in Athens are Hephaestion, the most preserved temple in Greece; the Agora, an ancient marketplace; the Keramikos, a cemetery begun in the 7th century BC; and the Stadium, a 4th-century BC site of games.

The Athens airport is important because it is strategically placed between the West and the Middle East. It has been the target of threats and bombings by terrorists.

Greeks in North America

From 1951-71, about 25% of Greece's work force went to the US, Canada, West Germany, Switzerland, and Australia. Most sent money home to Greece, and many returned finally to live in Greece. The number of Greeks emigrating in the past 10 years has dropped. In Canada, it dropped from 1,960 in 1977 to 534 in 1985. In the US it dropped from 7,838 in 1977 to 2,512 in 1986. But more Greeks are visiting North America — whether for business, government, or recreation. Greeks in America often send money for these trips, just as they send money so poor relatives in Greece can live more comfortably.

A Glossary of Useful Greek Terms

efcharisto (ef-hah-ree-STO) . . . . thank you
mitera (mee-TEH-rah) . . . . mother
oktapodi (oak-tah-POE-dee) . . . . octopus; popular seafood in Greece

60

parakalo (pah-rah-kah-LO) .... please
patera (pah-TEH-rah) .... father
psito chirino (psee-TOE hee-ree-NO) .... roast pork
souvlakia (suv-LAH-key-ah) .... seasoned meat grilled on a skewer
tin thalasa (teen THAH-lah-sah) .... the ocean
ti kanete (tee KAH-neh-teh) .... how are you?
yiasas (YEEAH-sas) .... hello

More Books about Greece

Here are some more books about Greece that may help you do research for the "Things to Do" projects. Check to see if your library has them.

Twelve Months. Aliki (Greenwillow)
Greece. Antoniou (Silver)
The Greeks. Crosher and Strongman (Silver)
Olympic Games in Ancient Greece. Glubok and Tamarin (Harper and Row)
Tales of Greek Heroes. Green (Penguin)
Faber Book of Greek Legends. Lines (Faber and Faber)
An Ancient Greek Town. Rutland (Watts)

Things to Do — Research

Greece and Turkey have fought for years. Thousands of people have died in their wars. Today, the issues are oil rights in the Aegean and the future of Cyprus. As you read about relations between Greeks and Turks, watch for current facts. Two library publications that will help you find recent information are

The Reader's Guide to Periodical Literature
Children's Magazine Guide

For answers to questions about such topics as ownership of the oil in the Aegean, look up *Greece* in these two publications. You will be sent to recent articles.

1. People have studied Greek architecture for centuries. Three kinds of columns that held the roofs of the temples were the Corinthian, the Doric, and the Ionic. Find out more about these columns. Look in encyclopedias and books about art history under the words *Greece, Greek architecture, Doric, Ionic,* and *Corinthian.*

2. Some of the most interesting stories in the history of literature are about the gods and goddesses of Greek myth mentioned in the "Religion" section. Learn more about them by looking in encyclopedias and books about religions and myths.

3. Alexander the Great was a famous military man. Find information about his 13-year campaign to capture lands for Greece. Good places to start looking are encyclopedias, books about Greek history, and books about military campaigns.

4. Imagine yourself as a child who lives on one of the islands of Greece or in a mountain village. What would your school be like? What would you do for medical care? How would your parents support you? What would you do after school and on weekends?

More Things to Do — Activities

These projects may help you learn more about Greece. You can do these projects at home or at school.

1. In research exercise one, you were asked to read about Doric, Ionic, and Corinthian temple columns. Many North American buildings have columns or column-like designs that look like those from ancient Greece. In your neighborhood and downtown area, notice what columns are like and see which style they resemble. Some buildings you might start with are churches, courthouses, or government offices. Many plain homes in small towns also have porch supports that resemble the ancient Greek column styles. Try copying some of the columns out of encyclopedias and drawing some porch posts you see.

2. Try writing some words using the Greek alphabet. In the "Language" section of this book you will find letters that are different from letters in our alphabet.

3. If you would like a pen pal in Greece, write to these people:

> International Pen Friends
> P.O. Box 65
> Brooklyn, New York 11229

Tell them the country you want your pen pal to be from and be sure to include your full name and address.

"Yiassas fili mou." (yee-AH-sas FEE-lee moo)
Goodbye, my friends.

Index